WHY BERT'S NOT A CHRISTIAN

WHY BERT'S NOT A CHRISTIAN

A CONVERSATION WITH SKEPTICS

BEN YOUNG

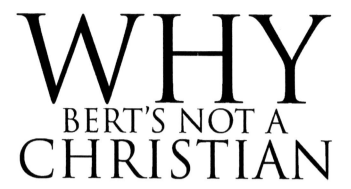

© 2004 by Ben Young. All rights reserved

Packaged by Pleasant Word, PO Box 428, Enumclaw, WA 98022. The views expressed or implied in this work do not necessarily reflect those of Pleasant Word. The author(s) is ultimately responsible for the design, content and editorial accuracy of this work.

No part of this publication may be reproduced, stored in a retrieval system or transmitted in any way by any means—electronic, mechanical, photocopy, recording or otherwise—without the prior permission of the copyright holder, except as provided by USA copyright law.

Unless otherwise noted, all Scriptures are taken from the Holy Bible, New International Version, Copyright © 1973, 1978, 1984 by the International Bible Society. Used by permission of Zondervan Publishing House. The "NIV" and "New International Version" trademarks are registered in the United States Patent and Trademark Office by International Bible Society.

Scripture references marked KJV are taken from the King James Version of the Bible.

Scripture references marked NASB are taken from the New American Standard Bible, © 1960, 1963, 1968, 1971, 1972, 1973, 1975, 1977 by The Lockman Foundation. Used by permission.

ISBN 1-4141-0324-7
Library of Congress Catalog Card Number: 2004098463

To my godly grandfather, G.B. "Buddy" Landrum
—Ben Young

Table of Contents

Acknowledgements 9

Chapter 1: Bert's Barbecue 11

Chapter 2: Because it's True for You,
    But Not for Me 19

    Do the Right Thing? 23
    No Escaping the Truth 25
    Go to the Source 27

Chapter 3: Because all Paths Lead to God 29

    What is Ultimate Reality? 30
    How Do You Handle Conflict? 32
    Relativism is a Religion 34

Chapter 4: Because all Christians are
  Hypocrites 37

  Just the Facts 37
  Leonardo and the Greeks 40
  Do Counterfeits Nullify the Genuine? 42

Chapter 5: Because Evolution is True 45

  Back to School 45
  What is Evolution Anyway? 46
  In Darwin We Trust 48
  Dissenting Voices 51
  Faith vs. Science? 56
  Learning from a Four-Year-Old 58
  What's Your Starting Point? 59

Chapter 6: Because the Bible is
  Full of Myths 61

  Not the Stuff Legends are Made of 62
  Do You Believe in Miracles? 63
  Have Monks Morphed the Texts? 65
  Who is Your Ultimate Authority? 67

Chapter 7: Back to Barbecue 69

Notes 81
Recommended Reading 85

Acknowledgements

I want to thank Sarah Welch and Toni Richmond for making this book a reality. Sarah made the book flow and wrote the big debates between Bert and Earnest. Toni championed this project from the get-go and made sure it went to press on time.

I also want to thank the late Dr. Gregory Bahnsen, Dr. Peter Kreeft, Paul Copan, Dr. Frank Harber, Dr. William Dembski, and Dr. Jim Tour for their great contribution to apologetics and to this book.

CHAPTER 1

Bert's Barbecue

One Sunday afternoon Earnest went to his favorite barbecue restaurant to eat what he considered one of the best brisket sandwiches on earth—the tenderest meat covered in sumptuous sauce on a toasted bun, with pickles, white onion, and loads of jalapeños. Even more appealing was the price; at $4.50 a pop, a great sandwich turns divine. So in he walked, Tums in tow. Just as he made it to the counter he heard a familiar voice over his shoulder: "Hey, it's 'Earnest,' right?" the voice asked. He turned around and tried his best to conceal his disappointment: "Yes, how are you, Bert?" He had been looking forward to an afternoon of anonymity, a time to just relax and not talk much, especially not to people from work. "Oh, fine. How's that project coming along?" Bert asked. "Almost done. What about yours?" Earnest said, stifling a sigh. Bert thought a second and then said with a chuckle: "It's the week-end, what am I doing talking about work?" In relief, Earnest let out that sigh he had stifled. "Maybe this won't be so bad," he thought. (Little did he know what was in store for him.) Bert and Earnest got their food at the same time and decided to join each other at one of the tables outside. Let's take a look at their conversation and see why heartburn ended up being the least of poor Earnest's worries that day:

> Bert – "So why are you dressed up?"
>
> Earnest – "I went to church this morning."
>
> Bert – "Church? I didn't know you were religious."
>
> Earnest – "Yeah, I've been going to church for a long, long time."
>
> Bert – "Interesting. So I had no idea you were a Bible-thumper," he chuckles.
>
> Earnest – "Well, I'm not . . . I mean . . . I'm not into pushing my beliefs on others."
>
> Bert – "Good for you, man! I get so tired of those folks who feel the need to convert everybody. I think it just shows weakness on their part. People need to keep their religious views to themselves, don't you think?"
>
> Earnest – "Well, I'm not sure about that."
>
> Bert – "It just seems like they're afraid to stand alone—almost like they need affirmation for what they believe. We all have our own in-

dividual beliefs. What's true and right for one person isn't necessarily true for the next."

Earnest – "Hmm. So what do you believe?"

Bert – "I personally believe that if you are a good person, you're going to be alright, whatever your idea of 'alright' is. We're all here just trying to do our best, you know? To me, it shouldn't matter what path you take. None of us really *knows* what the truth is anyway. And if there really is a God, I can't imagine Him condemning people to 'hell' for not believing one particular way. That just wouldn't be fair. It makes me so mad when these self-righteous Christians claim they're the only ones going to 'heaven.' You say you're a Christian—do *you* really believe that Jesus Christ is the only way to God?"

Earnest – "Yes, I do."

Bert – "So you would condemn all the Jews, Muslims, Hindus, and the rest of the moral population to hell just because they don't see Jesus as the Son of God?"

Earnest – "Yes, that is what the Bible says—Jesus *is* 'the way, the truth, and the life.' It's only through His blood that any of us can get to the Father. You see, it's all about God's grace, not our own works. The Bible says that "all have sinned and fallen short of God's glory" and that we're all in need of His grace. And, once we believe, we receive His Spirit, who enables us to live lives that are holy and pleasing to God. But it's only by His Spirit, see?"

Bert – "So, bottom line, if I don't believe in all this Jesus stuff, then *God*, if He even exists, is going to send me to the ultimate barbecue pit?"

Earnest – "If that's the way you want to put it, yes."

Bert – "Actually, that's the way you put it with your narrow-minded view. I suppose now you're trying to convert me . . . to rescue me from my ultimate doom. Ha! I thought you said you weren't into that sort of thing."

Earnest – "What sort of thing?"

Bert – "At the beginning of this discussion you said you weren't into pushing your beliefs on others, and now look what you're doing. It shouldn't surprise me—I've yet to meet a Christian who wasn't a hypocrite."

Earnest – "Now wait a minute, that's not fair, Bert . . ."

Bert – "What do mean, 'not fair'? I don't think it's fair when you Christians say the rest of us are going to 'hell' for not believing the way you do. How can you be so arrogant as to claim that your way is the only way?"

Earnest – "I don't know. I just know what I believe. I've put my faith in what the Bible says."

Bert – "Look, Earnest, any educated person knows that the Bible isn't really true. Evolution proved that a long time ago. I've read my fair share of the Bible, and, sure, we can glean a modicum of wisdom from its tales and proverbs, just like any other ancient writing, but do you honestly think that all that stuff really happened? The Bible is basically a bunch of myths. My grandmother was a Christian, and she used to tell us stories from the Bible. Let me ask you: How is a talking donkey plausible? (That one was my personal favorite.)"

Earnest – "First of all, I don't care about what scientists say about evolution. Science has been one of Satan's tools for many years. Second, the donkey really did talk. Haven't you ever heard of a miracle?"

Bert – "Miracles like that don't happen these days, and if they don't happen now, why would they have happened then? And another thing: How do you account for all those different authors and translations and such? There's no way we can give credibility to a work that's been passed around and undoubtedly embellished through the years."

Earnest – "I don't know. I just know that what I feel in my heart is true."

Bert – "How can you rest your whole belief system on your subjective feelings, Earnest? I feel in my heart that the world is flat. How do you feel about that?"

Earnest – "Everyone knows the world is not flat. That's been proven wrong."

Bert – "Proven by whom? Those Satanic scientists?"

Earnest – "Come on, Bert . . . you know what I mean."

Bert – "No, I don't know, and that's what really irks me. Earnest, you are a bright guy and a hard worker. I just can't figure out why you would believe all this mess when you know rationally that it's not true. Why do so many Christians feel the need to park their brains every time they go to church or open the Bible? I just don't get it."

Earnest – "You see, Bert, that's your problem. It takes faith. Sure all those questions about evolution, miracles, the Bible, and other people's religions bother me at times. So what? All those skeptics and doubters are probably wrong."

Bert – "Prove it!"

Earnest – "I can't prove it. I just know what I believe, and that's good enough for me."

Bert – "I just can't believe in something that doesn't make sense rationally. We live in a modern age with computers, cell phones, and microwaves, and how smart people like you can take this archaic blind leap of faith is beyond me. Speaking of blind, you spilled a little barbecue sauce on your tie there, Ernie."

Earnest – "Thanks, Bert."

Have you ever had a conversation like that? In your opinion, who won this informal debate? Although I was pulling for Earnest, I do believe that Bert came out on top here. He appeared to have a number of good reasons not to believe in God, the Bible, and Christ's claim to be the "way, the truth, and the life" (John 14:6), and Earnest didn't seem to have the answers for this array of religious and philosophical questions. He just wasn't ready. Would you be ready to respond to questions about your own belief system? Yes, you do have a belief system (all of us do), regardless of what it may be.

I can remember talking with one of my friends in college who happened to be a Hindu. During the course of the conversation, we both realized that I knew more about Hinduism than he did, and he had no way to defend his faith. We couldn't go any further with the discussion until he had gone and learned more about what he "believed." I don't know about you, but that is definitely not the kind of situation I relish being in. The truth is that we should all be able to answer this question for ourselves: "What is the basis for my beliefs, and how do those beliefs affect the way I live?" As humans, it is so natural for us to think that we have everything figured out. As Americans, we love to exercise our rights to talk about it. We all like a good debate over a *grandé mocha*, with Ella crooning in our ears, but when it comes to our primary belief system, a few quips we memorized in freshman humanities will not suffice. That's what this book is about. It's about intellectual integrity, about honesty, and about getting real with what you really believe.

If you are like Bert, a sincere skeptic looking for some answers, then I'm glad you've picked up this book. In the following chapters, I will respond to the many questions Bert posed in this debate, and, hopefully, you'll at least find these responses rational, if not altogether convincing. If you are more like Earnest, a sincere Christian in need of some intellectual artillery, then I'm glad you're reading this as well. I hope that in the chapters which follow, you will, one, come to understand why some people reject the Christian faith and, two, learn how you can respond more effectively to their objections. In the final chapter, we'll take a trip back to the barbecue joint and see how Earnest fares with more knowledge under his belt.

CHAPTER 2

Because it's True for You, But Not for Me

George Barna recently conducted a survey which showed that 64% of American adults (18 years old and up) do not believe in absolute and objective moral truth. He also found that 54% of adults who call themselves "born-again Christians" affirm some type of relativism in their beliefs.[1] In brief, relativism is a perspective which states that any particular point of view is equally as valid as all other points of view and that it is up to the individual to decide what he or she considers truth. If you subscribe to this philosophy and consider yourself to be a relativist, then please allow me to challenge you to rethink your claims.

Meet Frank and Carl. Frank owns a jewelry store; Carl is a diamond thief. However, Frank isn't aware of the fact that Carl is a thief. It's a typical morning at the store, and at about 10 A.M., Frank begins polishing some necklaces. Carl strolls in, feigning an interest in buying something for his wife. They talk about possible purchases for Carl, just as they've done everyday for the past week. Then Frank says:

"You know, I was watching Donahue last night, and they had some religious fanatic on there. This wacky fundamentalist was saying that he believes there is absolute truth. And, to top it off, he said that he knew this absolute truth and was trying to impose his beliefs and his morality on everyone else. Now, that just doesn't make any sense to me. How can one man claim to *know* the truth? How can one man say he has all the answers? What arrogance!"

> Carl – "Yeah, I know what you mean. I grew up in the church and heard that all the time. My mom was the worst . . . she was always trying to shove religion and the Bible down my throat. But, thank *God* (ha!), I've moved past all that."
>
> Frank – "I mean, everyone knows today that all truth is basically relative. It all depends on your culture and individual background. How can one culture say it's right and another is wrong? There is no absolute right and wrong. What truly enlightened person believes that?
>
> Carl – "I'm right there with ya, buddy."

Carl says he has a meeting and leaves without making a purchase yet again. He's been casing out the joint for a week now, and tonight he's ready to make his move. At 10 P.M., Carl routinely makes his way past the alarm, without a glitch. He's got his ski mask and a Glock 33 (with a silencer), and everything is going as planned except for one thing—there is a light on in the back. "Frank's not usually here at this time; I need to make sure," he thinks. He walks to the back, and, sure enough, Frank is sitting there, paying bills. In terror, Frank immediately yells out: "Hey, don't shoot . . . don't shoot . . . don't kill me . . . you can take whatever you want!"

> Carl – "That's exactly what I intend to do."
>
> Frank – "Hey, wait a minute. Don't I know you? I recognize your voice. You're Carl."
>
> Carl – "Frank, buddy, you shouldn't have done that. Now you've shown you know who I am, and if you know who I am, you'll turn me in, and if you turn me in, I'll have to go to jail, and I don't want to do that. So, Frank, it looks like I'm going to have to kill you."
>
> Frank – "You can't kill me! It's not right!"
>
> Carl – "Wait, wait, what do you mean 'it's not right'? You told me today that you don't believe in absolute right and wrong. It depends on the individual, right? So, I'm going to have to kill you. I have no choice; I've got to look out for myself."

Frank – "But I've got a wife and kids . . . I've got to take care of them."

Carl – "Your wife and kids will get insurance money and will probably be better off without you. But what do I care about that anyway? I have to do this. I can't trust you, Frank."

Frank – "Oh you can trust me. Look, I won't turn you in. Trust me, please. Take everything I have . . . I don't care . . . please just spare my life."

Carl – "Frank, you just don't get it. Remember our conversation today? Do you remember what you said, 'There's no such thing as right and wrong'? How can I trust you? What does your word mean? Tonight it's right for you to say you won't turn me in because it benefits you in this moment, but tomorrow it may be right for you to turn me in because you no longer have a gun to your head and you want your stuff back. Well, I'm doing what's right for me here. I'm not going to spend the rest of my life in the slammer, wearing an orange jumpsuit. I'm sorry, Frank." (He slowly squeezes the trigger, leaving Frank no time to recant his relativistic stance.)[2]

DO THE RIGHT THING?

Now, this may be an extreme example to you, but indulge me a minute. If your motto is, "It's true for you, but not for me," then you've got to give Carl his due. You must give him permission to kill Frank. He has that right because self-interest rules the day in his mind. You may be thinking, "That is a stupid story. Anybody knows that killing is wrong." Well, why is killing wrong? Why does an objective standard of right and wrong all of a sudden apply when it comes to murder? "I feel that it is wrong," you may say. But Carl felt that it was right for him. You may say, "Well, it's against the law to steal and to kill. They voted and passed legislation for this. It's up to society to determine what's right or wrong." Okay, but what if I said to you that black people are inferior to white people and that a bunch of white people should take over the Royal Caribbean, go down to Africa, and bring some black people back with them to be their slaves? By now you're really thinking I'm a nutcase because *everyone* knows that slavery and murder are morally reprehensible. On what grounds are they wrong, though? You just told me that society determines what is right and what is wrong, and just a while back in our nation's history, *society* said that slavery was okay. *Society* also voted Adolph Hitler as Chancellor of Germany, giving him 90% of the popular vote. And after WWII when the Nazis were on trial for exterminating nearly twelve million innocents (half of which were

Jews), their defense was that they never broke German law. Does that sound like a reasonable defense to you? Should their heinous crimes have been dismissed under that kind of logic? Absolutely not. But you have no standard for objecting. **You cannot oppose theft, murder, slavery, genocide, pedophilia, or anything else that you would consider unjust if society or the law deems them acceptable. So if moral truth is merely a social construct, you inevitably will have oppression.**

You may be thinking, "Hitler's regime and slavery are two extreme examples. Nevertheless, we can take society out of it. My point is that no individual should impose his morals or religious values on another individual. You don't have the right to tell me what to believe." But don't you see that in saying that I don't have the right to impose my beliefs on you, you are imposing your beliefs on me by telling me what I shouldn't do?

Now before we drown in a sea of quasi-semantics, let me give you another scenario: There is a man jogging by himself through the park one night. As he passes through a more secluded area, he sees someone brutally raping a young lady. He says to himself, "Well, I don't agree with what this man is doing, but who am I to say that he is in the wrong?" Now, would a true relativist have any basis for condemning this jogger? I don't think so. After all, he was only respecting the values (or lack thereof) of the rapist. Now, I'm not saying that all relativists stand for murder, oppression, and rape. In fact, I believe that most relativists are philanthropic by nature. What I am saying is that they don't always realize the repercussions of their claims. The German philosopher Friedrich Nietzsche admitted these repercussions when he wrote that "the obliteration of God—and therefore, all objective standards for truth and morality—would usher in an age of nihilism, the rejection of all objective meaning in value. All that is left is the will to power, by which only the fittest survive."[3] What it comes down to is this: When you throw objective moral truth out the window, it's every man for himself, and the individual freedom that was intended is forfeited and replaced by chaos and abuse.

NO ESCAPING THE TRUTH

In reality, we can say that we're "true" relativists all we want, but when the chips are down and the gun is to our heads, we all believe in absolute truth. We shake our fists in anger at Osama bin Laden, the massacre of hundreds of schoolchildren in Russia, and our English teacher for giving us a D because she didn't like the color of our skin. Why? Because we know that there is a right and there is a wrong outside of anyone's personal opinions about it. Something in us cries out for justice. We can't escape it any more than we can escape our longing to have intimate connections with others. It's the way we've been created. Every person in every culture has been made in the image of God. Though we have fallen and have distorted that image, it is still there. And written on that image, though faintly perhaps, is a conscience endowed with the absolutes of who God is and what He requires of us. Paul talks about this in Romans 2:14–15. He is referring to the Gentiles, who did not grow up under the law as the Jews did, when he says,

> "Indeed, when Gentiles, who do not have the law, do by nature things required by the law, they are a law for themselves, even though they do not have the law, since they show that the requirements of the law are written on their hearts, their consciences also bearing witness, and their thoughts now accusing, now even defending them."

This passage proves that, by nature, we know what's right in God's eyes even if we haven't had it spelled out for us in the law. Earlier, in Romans 1:20–21, he says:

> For since the creation of the world God's invisible qualities—his eternal power and divine nature—have been clearly seen, being understood from what has been made, so that men are without excuse. For although they knew God, they neither glorified him as God nor gave thanks to him, but their thinking became futile and their foolish hearts were darkened.

This passage hits the mark. We know what we are to do, but we don't always like to do it. God has revealed Himself to us through conscience, through nature, and through the Word, but we don't want to bend the knee to Him and proclaim that He is sovereign. We want to run our own lives. I struggle with this, and so does anyone else who's honest. There is a part of us that is drawn to God because we have an innate need to be in relationship with our Creator, yet there is another part of us that wants to run away from Him—a part that wants to create our own truths which fit into our own selfish agendas.

GO TO THE SOURCE

Here's what Jesus, God in the flesh, says about truth: "I am the Way, the Truth, and the Life" (John 14:6). **How can you find truth other than at its source? Any truth that does not have its foundation in a knowledge of God will eventually turn in on itself.** Relativism is a case in point. It sounds so appealing because it preaches tolerance and open-mindedness, but when you press it, it's a completely unlivable and self-contradictory worldview. Isn't the claim that there is no absolute truth an absolute truth claim in and of itself? For this very reason, it is at best confusing and at worst deceptive. Relativism may seem all encompassing, but it is just as exclusive as any other religious or philosophical perspective. Someone who believes in relativism cannot help but be just as dogmatic as someone who espouses Christianity or any other religion. It's impossible to avoid being emphatic about our particular belief system because (hopefully) everything in our lives—

our thoughts, decisions, and actions—is based on or affected by our beliefs. All I'm asking for is a little consistency, a little integrity here, which is the same that I ask for myself. If I claimed to follow Christ but lived my life as though I didn't, with absolutely no conviction about it, you would think I was a huge hypocrite. Indeed, I would be. So if you really don't believe in an absolute right or wrong, then please don't have an opinion about the way others have lived their lives, whether they are Charles Manson or Mr. Rogers.

Questions to Consider

1. Before you read this chapter, what was your position on moral relativism? (In other words, did you believe in absolute truth?) Since reading, has your position changed? Why or why not?

2. What is your ultimate standard for morality?

3. Apply that standard to Nazi Germany and slavery.

4. In the end of the scenario with Frank and Carl, do you think Frank had a leg to stand on in his argument with Carl, given his particular stance on morality?

CHAPTER 3

Because all Paths Lead to God

Oprah Winfrey once said, "One of the biggest mistakes humans make is to believe that there is only one way. Actually, there are many diverse paths leading to what you call God."[1] This perspective, held by Oprah, Bert, and the majority of our society, seems to foster humility by saying, "My way is no better than your way." Religious relativism, like moral relativism, is attractive to many people because it appears to be indiscriminate—it appears to embrace all people of all faiths. Perhaps you adhere to some form of religious relativism and see it as a way to promote peace in the midst of bigotry and prejudice. Let's take a look at this point of view and its implications. Does religious relativism in fact solve the problem of intolerance or, like moral relativism, does it end up creating the very thing it criticizes?

WHAT IS ULTIMATE REALITY?

Let's take a look at a classic illustration of the "Three Blind Men and the Elephant." Now imagine there are three blind men standing around an elephant, trying to figure out what it is. The first blind man grabs on to its leg and says, "Ah, the elephant is like a tree." The second blind man then comes and grabs hold of its tail and says, "No, no, you're wrong. The elephant is like a snake." Then the third blind man goes and leans on the side of the elephant. He says, "No, both of you are wrong. The elephant is not like a tree, nor is it like a snake. It is like a wall." Relativists often use this illustration to explain that all the religions of the world only grasp bits and pieces of the truth. In essence, those who hold to this view are saying that all people of faith are leaning up against the same ultimate reality or god but simply describe it in different ways, according to their various perspectives. If this argument were true it would certainly neutralize any of the absolute truth claims of Hinduism, Buddhism, Islam, Christianity, Judaism, or what have you. I would use this analogy if I were a religious relativist because it does sound really humble. If we're really all blind, someone who says, "I am the Way, the Truth, and the Life," would appear to be quite arrogant.

But take a behind-the-scenes look at this story, and some simple questions begin to surface: Who is telling the story, and what is his perspective? Obviously, the person telling the story is someone who can see the whole elephant. How else would he know that the three blind men are grasping only parts of it? How would he know that its leg is not a tree but only part of the elephant's body, or that the tail is merely the tail and not a snake, and so on? The storyteller is claiming to be at an exclusive vantage point that allows him to see ultimate reality. In other words, he alone gets the big picture. He knows what the elephant is and what the blind men are trying to figure out. All of a sudden, the storyteller doesn't sound so humble anymore, does he? You start asking a few questions, and you'll soon discover that his view is completely self-contradictory too. While he is claiming that there is not *one* correct path, he's establishing his own path, or understanding of it all, as the absolute standard.[2] There will be more on this shortly, but let's look at another popular way to describe religious relativism. It is what I like to call the Mountaintop Analogy. It states basically that God is at the top of a mountain and everyone else is at the bottom. As there are many different ways to the top of a mountain—some more difficult or time-consuming than others—so there are many different religions that all lead to the same God. Once again, we could ask the question: Who's describing this? How does he know that all paths reach to the top of the mountain unless he, himself, is at the top? Just like the storyteller of the three blind men and the elephant scenario, he is claiming to have absolute knowledge.

While we're at it, let's push his claim a little further. Would this relativist really say that every path leads to God? How about Hitler's? David Koresh's?

The KKK's? Most would say that these people are sociopaths and bigots, and I would have to agree. However, for a religious relativist to be consistent, he would have to say, "Yes, their ways lead to God as much as the next person's." He's not going to say that though. In Bert-like fashion, he'll say that what matters is being a "good" person. Well, where does the standard for what's "good" or "bad" come from if there is no such thing as absolute truth? He may say that standard is what we're taught. By whom, I'd ask? By our parents and teachers. Okay, where did they get it? Society. Need I remind you of where society took us in chapter one—to Nazi Germany and slavery?

HOW DO YOU HANDLE CONFLICT?

Furthermore, if you say that it doesn't matter what your religion is because they all lead to the same place, you are seriously ignoring some obvious conflicts. For example, Christians teach that God is personal; Buddhists teach that god is impersonal; Muslims teach that there is only one god, Allah; Jews teach that there is only one God, but he most certainly is *not* Allah; Hindus teach that there are millions of gods. I could go on and on with the differences, but hopefully by now you're seeing that it is impossible for all of these doctrines to be true at the same time. Please allow me to illustrate with an example. Say you're walking in the park, and you come across a woman who is obviously pregnant. You ask her, "When's the baby due?" She replies, "In just three more months." Now you happen to be walking at a pretty good clip, and you've lapped her. Just imagine that when you approach her again, you ask the exact same question ("When's the baby due?"), but this time, she says, "I'm not pregnant, you jerk!" You say, "I just asked you the same question, and you said you were, so which is it? Are you pregnant or not?" She says, "Well, I'm both." Hopefully, I don't have to go into how ridiculous that would be. **No one can be pregnant and not pregnant at the same time. By the same token, God cannot be personal and impersonal at the same time. Jesus cannot be *just* a "good teacher" and God in the flesh at the same time. To look seriously at each of the world religions is to admit they are vastly different.**

So how does a religious relativist deal with the blatant conflicting truth claims among the various world religions? It's as though he takes out a giant blender and throws them all into it. He takes the beliefs of the Jewish people, the Muslims, the Christians, the Buddhists, the Hindus, and whatever else he wants to add and presses *grind*, *blend*, or *puree*, obliterating their uniqueness. What results is this bland concoction that is relativism. Though they claim to, relativists don't listen to the voices of others. They would show more of the respect they profess by recognizing the opposing truth claims of the different world religions rather than conforming these religions to their own relativistic grid.

In essence, religious relativism offends where it sought to embrace. I once took part in a PBS interfaith dialogue with a Buddhist monk, a Jewish Rabbi, and an Islamic layperson. As the discussion unfolded, we discovered that we had some agreement in terms of morality, but we recognized that we had radically different belief systems and cordially agreed that we disagreed. If you are reading this and you consider yourself to be a religious relativist, please do not force us into your blender. Do not do violence to that which we hold sacred. Let us disagree in peace. We can handle it, I assure you.

RELATIVISM IS A RELIGION

Not only does religious relativism offend where it sought to embrace, but it also ends up creating the very thing it is criticizing. While relativists are busy denouncing absolute truth claims, they are simply making their own. Relativism is "the way, the truth, and the life" to them, and they expect all the religions of the world to bow down and act in deference. They are just as dogmatic about all paths leading to God as someone who believes in just one way. They can be just as intolerant and just as judgmental too. You'll never find a *true* relativist who authentically embraces the various faiths of the world. Religious relativism is a distinct religion in and of itself—case closed.

Perhaps by now you're thinking, "Well, if religious relativism doesn't really pan out when you analyze it, and if all paths can't lead to God, then what is the correct path?" Knowing that I'm a preacher, you've probably already guessed where this is going, but I challenge you to hear me out here.

Why the Christian path? What makes it different? Herein lies the distinction between the Christian path and all the rest: All the other paths are man's attempts to get to God; **Christianity is all about God's initiative**. God built a bridge for us. We don't have to build it. And He didn't just build it, He also (through Christ) provided the means by which we traverse it. It makes perfect sense when you really think about it. If God is sovereign and all-powerful, as most religions assert, wouldn't it necessarily follow that He would have to be the one to initiate the path? For the same reason, wouldn't it also follow that He would be the One enabling us to cross it?

When you dig deeply enough you see that all other paths/religions are based on man's effort to earn acceptance. But in Christianity, God's path is available to everyone, not just to those who "behave" (talk about tolerance). If I were to die today I would deserve eternal punishment and separation from God, but I can rest assured that He is not judging me on my own righteousness but on the righteousness of another—His very own Son (Romans 3:21–24). Jesus Christ lived a perfect life, then went to the cross and died a sinner's death so that man could receive His righteousness by simply trusting in Him. This indiscriminate acceptance is all because of God's grace. **You see, grace is not just getting something you and I do not deserve, it's getting the very opposite of what we, in fact, do deserve. Grace is what gives hope to the hooker as well as to the holy-roller.** Can you think of a better path than that?

So if there is a sovereign God, and there is, and if He has taken the initiative and has provided a way for us to know him, and He has, wouldn't it be the height of arrogance for us as mere human beings to reject this path and devise our own?

Questions to Consider

1. Before reading this chapter, did you believe that all paths were equally valid routes to the same destination or God?

2. After having read the chapter, has your position changed? Why or why not?

3. Explain how relativism ends up creating the very thing it criticizes.

4. What distinguishes the Christian path from all the others?

CHAPTER 4

Because all Christians are Hypocrites

JUST THE FACTS

If you're at all like I am, you're greatly anticipating the end of "reality" TV. I must admit, however, I wasn't always so jaded. The first attempt at a reality show that I remember was *Dragnet* with Jack Webb and Harry Morgan, and it was actually one of my favorite shows. The acting was terrible, but the show always fascinated me. My favorite character was Sergeant Joe Friday, the lead cop in the series. He was tough and to the point. Oftentimes he questioned various people on the show to get information regarding a case. Whenever one of them would start to go off on a tangent, he would interrupt and say, "Please, ma'am . . . nothing but the facts." Well, that's just what this chapter is going to be. We're going to pull a Sgt. Friday and demand nothing but the facts about hypocrisy. Perhaps the biggest fact we need to just lay out there is this: There are hypocrites in the church, and if you're turned off by them, you're in *good* company.

I was born and raised in the church. My dad has been in the ministry for about 40 years now, my older brother has for 20, and I have for about 18. **During these decades I've seen incredible degrees of hypocrisy. I'm talking about Bible-toting-fish-on-the-bumper-hallelujah-speaking-WWJD- wearing people who finally showed their true colors, and they weren't pretty.** I've known hypocrites, believe me, and I hate hypocrisy as much (maybe even more, given what I've seen) as you do. Okay, that said, let's go over some more facts about hypocrisy.

Fact#1: Jesus Christ hates hypocrisy. When He was on this earth, He was constantly at war with hypocrites. Take a look at Matthew 23:27–28:

> Woe to you, teachers of the law and Pharisees, you hypocrites! You are like whitewashed tombs, which look beautiful on the outside but on the inside are full of dead men's bones and everything unclean. In the same way, on the outside you appear to people as righteous but on the inside you are full of hypocrisy and wickedness.

Those are some pretty tough words, wouldn't you say? There's a lot more where that came from. Just read the rest of Matthew, along with Mark, Luke, and John, and you'll see that a huge chunk of the Gospels is devoted to Christ's many diatribes against hypocrisy, most of which were directed right at the main culprits of the day—the Pharisees. These "holy-rollers" thought their religiosity would put them in good standing with God. They couldn't have been more wrong. Granted, all of us fall short in our own efforts, but what was so unbearable about these prigs was their claim to such piety. Jesus gives a whole list in Matthew 23 of ways in which they fell short of the Law they professed to hold so dear. He continually raged with a righteous anger against these men in order to wake them up from their hypocritical slumber. So, as I said earlier, if hypocrites make you angry, you are in *good* company—the very best, in fact.

Fact#2: Hypocrites happen. And they happen in all sorts of places, not just in the church. It just so happens, though, that the church is where they seem the most offensive. In reality, we shouldn't be so shocked by their presence; we received fair warning. Christ specifically said we would find them there and told us to be on our guard, saying that there would be many wolves dressed in sheep's clothing. John, one of Christ's closest followers, also predicted that false teachers and hypocrites would infiltrate the church. Paul mentioned them as well in his letters, encouraging those new in the faith to be on their guard and watch out for folks who appear to be harmless but are actually out to work their wickedness. There have always been hypocrites and backstabbers in the church, and there always will be. One doesn't need a PhD in church history to know of the many atrocities committed by people who called themselves Christians. To name just a few: the Spanish Inquisition, the Salem witch trials, the different scandals in the 80s involving some famous (now infamous) televangelists, and the more recent—or more *public*, I should say—child molestation scandals with the Catholic priests.

Hypocrisy in the church has been an ever-present anathema to anyone involved. I know there are many people who have been hurt and abused by someone in a church setting or someone who called himself/herself a Christian. Perhaps I'm speaking directly to you, dear reader. Maybe you were forced to do something you knew wasn't right or were made to jump through some religious hoop. Maybe you were embarrassed somehow. **Only you truly know the damage that's been done to your heart and soul, and you know all too well that no human can make it right. It will take a work of God. Know that He is willing and wanting to do so.** Please just let me say this: As someone who has grown up in the church and as someone who is seeking to follow Christ, I apologize. I'm sorry for the initial blow and the pain that followed. I'm sorry for the mistrust you feel now because of it. Know that Jesus is on your side. Know that He will take care of you, and He will also deal with the one who hurt you. In the meantime, He says to be on our guard.

LEONARDO AND THE GREEKS

Fact#3: "Sinner" does not equal "hypocrite." This is one of the most crucial facts to see (along with

Fact#1). There is a definite distinction between someone who is a hypocrite and someone who is just a sinner. A hypocrite is someone who pretends to be something he is not. The word "hypocrite" comes from the Greek word *hypokrites*, which basically means, "to play a part." Remember in the glory days of the Greek theater when only one or two actors would perform an entire play? It didn't matter how many characters were in the play, these actors could pull it off because they had a variety of masks to wear. Well, they were called "hypocrites." Or perhaps you saw the movie *Catch Me if You Can* a couple of years ago. In this movie Leonardo DiCaprio's character is a hypocrite, in the literal sense, who poses as a pilot for PanAm, a medical doctor, as well as a lawyer. Jesus called the Pharisees hypocrites because they tried to mask their true identities with a righteous façade and were less concerned with the state of their hearts and minds.

A sinner, on the other hand, is someone who breaks God's Law and falls short of His standard of perfection. One of the prerequisites for being a Christian is admitting that you are a sinner. It wouldn't make any sense for "sinner" and "hypocrite" to be synonymous because no religion would have hypocrisy as a prerequisite. (If there is a church with this prerequisite, please tell me where it is so that I can stay as far away from it as possible.) Paul, who wrote thirteen books of the New Testament, called himself the "worst of sinners," and yet he vehemently denounced hypocrisy. Remember, a hypocrite is someone who pretends to be someone he is not. Paul, obviously, did not fit this description. He recognized that he was a sinner in need of God, as all of us are.

So what exactly is a Christian? **A Christian is a sinner who is actively seeking to eradicate any duplicity present in his or her life.** Allow me to explain: If you are a Christ follower, then God accepts you on behalf of Christ's sacrifice and declares you righteous. You have been given a new, righteous identity that is independent of anything you can do (or not do, even). Because this new identity is independent of your behavior, it is still possible for Christians to sin, and most do every day in thought, word, or deed. So, as a Christian, you acknowledge the sin inside of you and you seek to live up to your *true identity* in Christ by daily (even "momently") confessing, by praying, by studying God's Word, and by seeking to please Him in all that you do. Therefore, we can easily conclude that all Christians are sinners, but not all Christians are necessarily hypocrites.

DO COUNTERFEITS NULLIFY THE GENUINE?

Even so, if you're still thinking, "Well, *most* Christians I've come across were hypocrites, so I don't want to have anything to do with Christianity," I want to challenge you to think about this question: Does the presence of counterfeits nullify the genuine? In other words, because there are hypocritical Christians in the church, can none be authentic or genuine? Let's go back to Leonardo in *Catch Me if You Can* and see if he sheds light on the subject. Because his character was posing as a pilot for PanAm, does that mean there are no real, certified pilots in that airline? What about medical doctors? Since he pretended to be one, does that mean all doctors are quacks and phonies? What if I showed you a counterfeit $50 bill? Would you turn down the one your grandfather gives you for Christmas because all $50 bills are suddenly counterfeit? Take Picasso prints. Do they nullify authentic Picasso paintings? Or take cubic zirconium. Because there are manmade diamonds, are there no genuine stones that come out of the ground anymore? Say you read an article on crooked cops. I bet you'll still call 9-1-1 if someone is breaking into your house. Am I wrong? Hopefully, you're getting my point. In fact, this argument simply turns in on itself when you press it because there necessarily has to be an authentic in order for there to be a counterfeit of it.[1]

So now we come to the real question: Is your claim that all Christians are hypocrites a genuine reason for your not accepting Christianity, or is it just an excuse? If you're honest, you'll admit that it is more of an excuse than a genuine reason. I think there are a lot of people who use this excuse, and many others like it, as part of a defense mechanism. It prevents them from having to deal with the real issue, which is not who and what Christians are but who and what Jesus Christ is. **Jesus Christ is not a**

hypocrite, and you'll be hard-pressed to find someone even in the atheist or agnostic camp who would deny that He walked what He talked.

QUESTIONS TO CONSIDER

1. In general, which of the following do you believe?

    a) All Christians are hypocrites.

    b) Most people are hypocrites.

    c) People who think all Christians are hypocrites are simply trying to cover up a deeper issue.

    d) Hypocrisy is not unique to Christianity.

    Explain your answer.

2. Describe the difference between a hypocrite and a sinner.

3. If you believe that the church is full of hypocrites, is that belief based on a specific experience?

4. If so, have you held the entire church responsible for the actions of one or a few people who hurt you?

CHAPTER 5

Because Evolution is True

BACK TO SCHOOL

Not too long ago I had the opportunity to talk with Lee Strobel, who is one of the leading Christian apologists of our day. I asked him to tell me a little bit about his spiritual journey. He began his answer by recounting some experiences he'd had in his high school biology class. One experience, in particular, had affected him more than any other, and that was learning about Darwin and the theory of evolution. He remembered coming to the conclusion one day that if Darwin was right, then God was out of a job. After realizing in that moment that the two were irreconcilable, he trusted in Darwin and squelched any semblance of faith he'd had in God. From that point on, and through most of his adult life, he was an avowed atheist. Another former atheist named

Patrick Glynn had a very similar experience. Here's what he said about it:

> I embraced skepticism at an early age when I first learned of Darwin's theory of evolution in, of all places, Catholic grade school. **It immediately occurred to me that either Darwin's theory was true or the creation story in the Book of Genesis was true. They could not both be true,** and I stood up in class and told the poor nun as much. Thus began a long odyssey away from the devout religious belief and practice that had marked my childhood toward an increasingly secular and rationalistic outlook. I was not alone in this journey."[1]

Can you relate to these guys at all? Perhaps you began to connect the dots of evolution back in school, and your faith in a Creator (if you had faith to begin with) completely dissolved. Or maybe you do believe in God, but in your mind evolution does sound rational, and this bothers you. Perhaps you are scared to ask some of the questions you may have, for fear of compromising your belief in God. Whatever your stance, this chapter is going to give you some good mental jerky to chew on and will challenge you to really examine what you say you believe.

WHAT IS EVOLUTION ANYWAY?

First off, we need to define some terms and figure out what we mean when we are talking about evolution. There are all kinds of theories of evolution. Microevolution, macroevolution, and theistic evolution are among the most prevalent. Microevolution refers to change within a species. In other words, microevolution explains why we have various kinds of birds. On the other hand, macroevolution refers to change from species to species—a bird becoming a cat becoming a dog becoming a horse becoming an ape becoming a human. This is more commonly known as Darwinian evolution. Darwinian evolutionists say that there is no God, nor is there any kind of transcendent, supernatural, or spiritual realm in the universe. Instead, we live in a closed system, and all we have before us is matter and molecules in motion, or, as Carl Sagan put it in the introduction to his *Cosmos* series on TV, "The universe is all that is, or ever was, or ever will be." This is a completely naturalistic view. On the other hand, theistic evolutionists believe that there is no conflict between the biological process that Darwinian evolutionists assert and the book of Genesis. They simply say that God directs and guides the unfolding of all the different life forms through the course of millions of years.

There is one last theory I want to add called intelligent design. Those who hold to this theory point to various complex biological structures, such as the eye and birds' wings and say that these could not possibly have developed by purely random mutations and, instead, necessitate a designer, though they do not specify who or what this designer is.

They concede that certain forms of microevolution provided the mechanism by which this intelligent designer created the various species. Some, not all, champions of this theory also believe in speciation (the creation of more than one species out of a single species).[2] Though, as stated above, this intelligent designer is not specified as the God of the Bible, there are, in fact, many Christians who hold to this theory. Dr. Michael Behe is one of them. You can check out Behe's book, *Darwin's Black Box*, to get a much better idea of what the intelligent design movement is all about.

IN DARWIN WE TRUST

Now that we've defined our terms, I'd like to address macro- or Darwinian evolution because it is what's implicit in the title of this chapter, as well as whenever the average person is talking about "evolution." What Charles Darwin basically said was that the cosmos and everything we see in human beings and animals are the results of three things: matter, random chance, and a whole lot of time. And since 1859, when Darwin published his magnum opus, *The Origin of Species*, this explanation has basically ruled the day in academia. So when you look at major intellectual and cultural influencers in the Western world—those in the grade schools, the universities, the graduate level classes, in many popular forms of media, as well as in literature—you will find that the vast majority of them buy into some type of Darwinian evolution. It's not the only story in town, but it's the only story that is allowed, and it's been very effective in its conquest of the "educated mind." And its influence is not limited to fields of science. Darwin's ideas influenced Freud in a tremendous way, and, therefore, psychology and sociology as we know them draw their lifeblood in many ways from Darwinian evolution.

One of the main reasons this theory has had such an influence on the whole of Western thought is because it draws such bold conclusions and then conceals them in scientific, "neutral" language. You'll see this quite often in the realm of metaphysics, which is simply the study of reality. Any topic, no matter how unrelated to science it may be, is free game—whether it's love, the existence of God, or simply a philosophical perspective. For example, take a look at the following quote by the late evolutionary biologist, Stephen Jay Gould:

> We are here because one odd group of fishes had a peculiar fin anatomy that could transform into legs for terrestrial creatures; because comets struck the earth and wiped out dinosaurs, thereby giving mammals a chance not otherwise available . . . because a small and tenuous species, arising in Africa a quarter of a million years ago, has managed, so far, to survive by hook and by crook. We may yearn for a "higher" answer—but none exists. This explanation, though superficially troubling, if not terrifying, is ultimately liberating and exhilarating.[3]

Did you catch that? Gould is spouting off a few scientific assumptions (mind you, even the scientific parts are *assumed* here) in order to bring home his own philosophical viewpoint. What viewpoint is that? Existentialism—plain and simple. He's saying that we merely exist to exist and that there's no real purpose. What's so "exhilarating" to him is the freedom he thinks his viewpoint guarantees. If there is no purpose or authority (aside from himself, of course), he's completely "liberated" to do as he pleases. I'll give some similar yet bolder quotes later on in the book, but the bottom line here is that people have all sorts of agendas, and they'll use whatever means they can to rationalize their own lives and even to sell their ideas to you.

Take movies, for example. Many filmmakers (actually it's more like "most") have an agenda. They have a particular worldview or a life philosophy that they are seeking to educate you about or persuade you to get in on. You can find this in almost any movie from a Disney cartoon to a David Fincher production. Now, they won't come out at the beginning of their movie and say, "The following movie is going to give you an overview of the philosophical viewpoint of nihilism, originated by Friedrich Nietzsche in Germany." They use the medium of cinema to communicate their particular worldview in either a subtle or sometimes not-so-subtle way. Much in the same way, evolutionists can be sly in presenting what they have virtually no scientific basis for believing, much less teaching about, and they can get away with this because they mask their ideas in "scientific" jargon. This method seems to have worked for the last one hundred years in spite of the major problems and weaknesses within the Darwinian theory, but the holes are getting wider, deeper, and more and more exposed every day.

DISSENTING VOICES

I recently interviewed Dr. James Tour, who is currently the Chao Professor of Chemistry at Rice University's Department of Chemistry and Center for Nanoscale Science and Technology (CNST). He's done postdoctoral training at the University of Wisconsin, as well as at Stanford, and he has also served as a visiting scholar at Harvard. Dr. Tour's scientific research areas include molecular electronics, chemical self-assembly, conjugated oligomers, electroactive polymers, combinatorial routes to precise oligomers, polymeric sensors, flame retarding polymer additives, carbon nanotube modification and composite formation, synthesis of molecular motors and nanotrucks, use of the NanoKids concept for K-12 education in nanoscale science, and methods for retarding chemical terrorist attacks. He has received numerous prestigious awards and has more than two hundred publications with sixteen patents or published patent applications.[4] In our chat, I asked him this question: "Dr. Tour, what are some of the problems you see with the theory of evolution?" Here is what he said:

I have trouble with the Darwinian account because it doesn't fit; it doesn't fit the process in which molecular structure can change to build one entity and transform it into another, into another, into another. I don't see the process for the life generation. We [scientists] don't even understand what goes on in a cell. We don't even understand the little machinery that goes on. People say, "Well, we can clone" . . . .We do not understand what goes on in the nucleus of a cell to the degree that we need. We just can't understand it. The knowledge isn't there. I can't build a machine. I don't even know how to understand life on that basis. I had a group of scientists sit in my living room in front of my kids (I wanted them to see this), and I said, "Take a cell. You have a cell. And that cell just died. No more life. Can you bring it back to life? Everything is there. Everything is in place. Everything is there." And they started arguing about this. "Well, what really is life?" "It's ionic potential," one person said. And the microbiologist said, "No, no, it's much deeper than that." And I said, "You guys can't even define life for me. You can't even bring that little cell back that has everything in place. It just died, and you are going to tell me that you understand a whole lot about this?" And they said, "No, we understand very little." **Maybe the high school teacher understands a lot in their own mind, but when you really get to the details, you don't understand. I don't understand how we can have a theory, like Darwinian Theory, and start to build such a grandiose scheme with so little knowledge.**

In November, I had the opportunity to talk with another dissenting voice. That voice belongs to Dr. William Dembski, who is at the forefront of the intelligent design movement. He is a mathematician, a philosopher, and an author. Dr. Dembski has taught at Northwestern and Notre Dame. He has done postdoctoral work in mathematics at MIT, in physics at the University of Chicago, and in computer science at Princeton University. He is a graduate of the University of Illinois at Chicago, where he earned a BA in psychology, an MS in statistics, and a PhD in philosophy. Dr. Dembski also received a doctorate in mathematics from the University of Chicago and, for fun, a master of divinity degree from Princeton Theological Seminary.[5] Here is what he had to say about the whole issue of Darwinism and some of the weaknesses he sees within that particular theory:

> If you really look at it . . . there are some classes of biological problems, certain types of systems. A colleague of mine named Michael Behe calls them irreducibly complex systems. These are multi-part, integrated systems where everything has to be in place for the basic function to be obtained. And these things have just resisted any sort of evolutionary, naturalistic explanation (you know, where there is no sort of design involved in them). And the interesting thing is on the flipside we do know how systems like that arise. What has become really the mascot of the intelligent design movement is a little molecular

motor on the backs of certain bacteria. They are called bacterial flagella. They are basically, motor-driven, outboard, bi-directional propellers, and they move the bacterium through its watery environment; and these things spin at 20,000 rpm and change direction in a quarter turn. So they are spinning 20,000 rpm, and within a quarter turn, they are spinning 20,000 rpm in the other direction. Howard Berg at Harvard will call this the most efficient machine in the universe. He hasn't written this, but in public lectures he will call it that. You look at this under an electron micrograph, and it's a machine. The biologists will call them molecular machines. And you've got a driveshaft, you've got the propeller part, you've got a hook joint, you have something that mounts this whole thing on its cell wall so you have disks. You've got stators, rotors—it's a machine. Now, how do you get something like that? Well, in our experience, there is only one way we know of how these come about, and that's by design.

In talking with these men who work at the molecular level on a daily basis, the holes in the Darwinian theory become much more evident.

However, you don't have to be a scientist and have a zillion PhDs to have some intelligent questions about evolution. For example, the evolutionary theory cannot explain the mechanism of evolution. That's what both Dr. Tour and Dr. Dembski are getting at, though in different ways. It also cannot explain gaps in the fossil record that have been there since Darwin published *Origin* in 1859. Evolutionists cannot explain the appearance of matter. When you think about it, folks, logic tells us that someone or something has to be eternal; evolution cannot explain the eternality of matter. Evolution cannot explain how matter produced life. In other words, how could a non-living thing like this page produce a cricket? How did intelligence spring from non-intelligence? How did moral beings spring from something amoral? The truth is, evolution is just a *theory*, though it is falsely presented as fact most of the time. In order for something to be considered scientific fact, it has to be reproducible and testable; you can't reproduce and test evolution. In light of all these holes, it's puzzling to me how *religiously* the vast majority of scholars and academic types still cling to the theory of evolution. I mentioned my puzzlement to Dr. Tour, and this is what he said:

> **The number of people in academia that are really qualified to begin to think of some of these fundamental questions is a much smaller number. For example, there are social scientists that really are not experts in the science side, but they will hold to [the Darwinian theory] quite strongly. They will hold to this because they think that *somebody* knows, but I just want to know *that somebody* [who can] explain to me how you get these sequences in these amino acids. That's the level in which I work. I work at the molecular level. I spend years trying to put a particular organic moiety on a particular mol-**

ecule, with a particular orientation, with a specific handedness, because all these molecules are generally chiral, meaning they have non-superimposable mirror images. And we have tremendous trouble doing this when we can choose all sorts of solvent media, all sorts of temperature ranges, all sorts of metal-catalyzed reactions, whereas biological systems are restricted generally to aqueous media and, generally, to a small subset of elements that it has available. "Explain to me how you are satisfied by this," [I would say], and to those who understand the level that I am getting at, the problem becomes far more difficult to rationalize.

If you would like to explain that to Dr. Tour, I am sure you can go down to Rice some time this week or just send him an email. Right now you may be having flashbacks to chemistry or biology class, and you're starting to break out in hives. There will not be a pop test on non-superimposable mirror images at the end of this chapter. Don't worry.

FAITH VS. SCIENCE?

In the last forty or fifty years, we have been led to believe that there is this dichotomy between faith and science. In fact, I would say that most people in our mainstream culture would say you can't be a Christian and a scientist because Christians are people of faith and scientists are people of fact. I very much respect the intellectual integrity of scientists like Dr. Tour and Dr. Dembski, who are willing to admit the limitations of their endeavors and of science. Dr. Tour was speaking of things on the molecular level that can't be proven (that don't have a mechanism to explain them) when I asked him this question: "Dr. Tour, are you telling me then that it actually takes faith to believe in evolution?" This is what he said:

> Certainly, certainly you are going to need a lot of faith to believe in evolution, to go from step A to step B. And those who say it's no problem for them, I think, are really rookies. They don't understand because they feel that, "Oh, well scientists understand." **No, scientists really don't understand; not at this level, they don't. And they will look from a 30,000 foot level, and they say, "This changes into this changes into this." Well, that's a wonderful paradigm. Wonderful! But now let's get a little more detailed.** How did that change occur? If I just even begin to push that a little bit, as I would in any other field of endeavor: You put molecule A on the board, and you show me molecule B; what is the mechanism of that transformation? I expect that of a student, to show that to me. If they are going to say, "This is what I started with; this is what I got," then I say, "Propose to me some mechanism by which that molecule changed, the discreet steps," and if they can't, I have real trouble with their mechanism. I believe you have B. I believe you had A. But if you can't explain to me the mechanism based on something that begins to fit, that mechanism doesn't hold much water. We could probably disprove that.

So perhaps you are still saying that you believe in the theory of evolution in spite of what Dr. Tour and Dr. Dembski say. You, obviously, have every right to believe what you want. However, please realize that it takes just as much faith to believe in the theory of evolution as it does to believe in a God who created the universe and everything in it. In fact, according to Dr. Tour's and Dr. Dembski's perspectives, it takes a great deal more.

LEARNING FROM A FOUR-YEAR-OLD

Okay, let's come up for some air. I think we can learn a lot from my four-year-old daughter Claire. She has learned a behavior that is somewhat crafty and very practical for her. Whenever she gets in trouble for stealing her big sister's crayon or hitting her big sister, she will come to my wife or to me in her own defense, crying, "It was an accident," with crocodile tears streaming down her face. But, on the other hand, when something happens to Claire—maybe her big sister steals her crayon or hits her—she comes running to us, saying, "She did it on purpose." Something like this happened today, in fact. Now, you're probably wondering what in the world this has to do with our whole debate on the origins of life, but just hang with me. When you start whittling it all down, you'll see that the debate actually has very little to do with evolution; it even has very little to do with whether the earth is six days old or six billion years old. When we look at the debate between those who believe in an intelligent designer (whether that intelligent designer is the God of Scripture or some other god or force) versus those who believe in chance, you'll see that it was raging long before Darwin came on the scene in the 1800s and introduced the theory of evolution. This brings me back to my four-year-old. Claire unknowingly reduced the whole argument to two simple components—one represents accident; the other represents purpose. One believes in a designer, while the other believes in chance. Now, the idea of a designer sounds the most logical to me. If I were to find a nice, silver watch in the middle of the Swiss Alps, my absolute last guess would be that it was the product of random chance. No, I'd say, "Man, someone had to have designed this." And how much more complex is a snowflake, or your fingerprint, or the human eye, or a flower?

WHAT'S YOUR STARTING POINT?

Why do so many intelligent people (far more intelligent than I) disagree on this issue? How is it possible that Dr. Dembski and Dr. Stephen Hawking could be looking through the same microscope, at the same molecule, and Dembski will see intelligent design, and Hawking will see random chance? Ultimately, it all depends on your starting point. Your starting point, whatever it may be, will have a direct effect on the way you perceive data. If I am starting with a belief in a transcendent God and Creator, then everything—right down to the individual facts I perceive in the universe—will be viewed in light of this belief. By the same token, if I come from the perspective of philosophical naturalism, and I believe that we live in a closed system and that all we really have are molecules in motion, then, obviously, I'm going to interpret observations in a way that backs up my original assumption. Here's a practical illustration of the point I just made: Your view of your father oftentimes plays a part in your view of God (for better or for worse).

Let's take it a bit further and point out, however, that your earthly father isn't God. In fact, he's nothing like Him. My point? It is quite possible to be wrong in your original assumption. We'll talk more about ultimate starting points at the end of the next chapter. In the meantime, I hope you'll seriously consider the different perspectives on the theory of evolution and the idea of intelligent design that were presented here.

QUESTIONS TO CONSIDER

1. What is your position on evolution, creation, and intelligent design?

2. How does your answer to question one relate to your beliefs about the God of the Bible?

3. Do you separate people of faith from people of science? Why or why not?

4. Explain what non-superimposable mirror images are. Just kidding.

CHAPTER 6

Because the Bible is Full of Myths

Stan hated Christians. One of his favorite pastimes was daring God to strike him with a lightning bolt right there in the cafeteria to prove His existence. He would then revel in rubbing his perceived "victory" in the faces of his Christian onlookers. Confronting, mocking, you name it, and Stan embodied it. He actually went so far one day as to burn pages of the Bible in front of a group of Christians just to get a rise out of them. On one hand, you probably have no desire to use the Bible as kindling, as my friend Stan did, but on the other hand, you may have a number of reasons for rejecting the Bible as the true Word of God.

Perhaps you related to Bert's array of doubts about the credibility of the Bible. You may have found yourself in a similar conversation at one time, using what I call the 3M Approach: Myths, Miracles, and Monk-morphing.

NOT THE STUFF LEGENDS ARE MADE OF

First of all, if you were to say that the Bible is full of myths, I would have to ask you what you mean by the word "myth." If you have read the Bible and have studied classical literature at all, you have undoubtedly seen that the Bible is not written in a mythological format. Nor does it read like a fairytale, which is highly fanciful. It is a record of history which contains a wide variety of literary genres—biography, poetry, narrative, and eyewitness accounts. Let's look closely at one of these eyewitness accounts and see how realistic it is in nature. Take the account of the Pharisees and the adulteress. These self-righteous men throw her at the feet of Jesus and are testing Him to see if He will condemn this "obvious sinner." Instead of condemning her, the writer tells us that He quietly begins writing in the sand. This is exactly what a true eyewitness would tell us—details that he understood no more than we do. This is not the sort of detail that writers of legend put in their tales.

And what of the specific names and dates which pinpoint this story on an actual timeline? These are not characteristic of the vagueness of legends either. Consider all the little insights into character that we get in the Gospels, as well. Legends don't have such depth. What can we conclude then? If the Gospels are not genuine eyewitness accounts and are merely fantasy or legend, then not only did these Galilean commoners invent the biggest and most successful hoax in human history, but they also invented a completely unique and unparalleled literary form—the realistic fantasy.[1] **So if you are saying that you have a problem with the Bible because it seems mythical, then I believe what you're really saying is that you have a problem with the supernatural—the parting of the Red Sea, the virgin birth, the walking on water, and the raising of the dead (just to name a few).**

DO YOU BELIEVE IN MIRACLES?

One of Bert's reasons for rejecting the Bible as a reliable document was the presence of miracles. To quote him: "Miracles like that don't happen these days, and if they don't happen now, why would they have happened then?" In other words, "We now live in a modern, enlightened world, and everyone knows that miracles do not happen because they are contrary to the laws of nature." If you concur with Bert and reject the Bible because it contains miracles, please allow me to ask you a few questions.

- How do you know that miracles do not happen today? Let's think about this question for just a moment. How much information would you really need to make such a claim? How much data about the natural realm would you have to have at your disposal to know for a fact that miracles are impossible? The answer is obvious if you're intellectually honest with yourself: You would have to know ev-

ery conceivable fact of science to make the grandiose claim that a supernatural world does not exist.

- *How do you account for the immutable laws of nature, given your worldview?* In other words: How do you know that nature operates in a law-like manner? Perhaps you would answer that you know that nature obeys certain laws because you can see and test these laws. The first problem with that answer is this: Not all of nature is contained in your minute experience. In philosophical argumentation, you are guilty of a hasty generalization, which means that you are taking a tiny bit of evidence and universalizing it. The second problem is a little more complicated: If all you can know is what you can see and test, then you really can know very little. Why? Because you cannot be sure that the knowledge you take in at this present moment can be applied to the past or to the future. You may assume that it applies, but you cannot *know* because you can neither go back in time nor jump to the future to test it. This is one of the reasons atheistic philosopher David Hume said that we cannot see causation (the relationship between causes and effects). In other words, we cannot determine that A necessarily causes B simply because B happens to follow A at a given point in time. We can see that B may follow A most of the time, but we cannot possibly know that it always has or always will. We can learn a lot from Lisa Simpson about the difference between causation and mere correlation in this humorous demonstration which appeared in an episode of *The Simpsons* (Season 7, "Much Apu about Nothing"):

Homer: Not a bear in sight. The "Bear Patrol" must be working like a charm!
Lisa: That's specious reasoning, Dad.
Homer: Thank you, dear.
Lisa: By your logic, I could claim that this rock keeps tigers away.
Homer: Oh, how does it work?
Lisa: It doesn't work.
Homer: Uh-huh.
Lisa: It's just a stupid rock. But I don't see any tigers around, do you?
Homer: Lisa, I want to buy your rock.[2]

If you cannot see causation, then you cannot say with any authority that there are certain laws that nature has always and will always obey. Therefore, to reason that you can know that miracles are impossible simply because Mother Nature follows certain rules is completely arbitrary, given your inability to account for these rules. The truth is that in order to do science, math, or even think logically, you need an omniscient and omnipresent God who providentially controls and guides the universe in a predictable way. (Dr. Gregory Bahnsen uses this line of argumentation in his epic 1985 debate with Dr. Gordon Stein, the former editor of *Skeptic Magazine*.)

HAVE MONKS MORPHED THE TEXTS?

A common argument that Bert used to refute the reliability of the Bible was that monks "morphed" the text. Maybe you agree with him and would say to me: "How can you be sure the Bible you have today is the original? Surely the scribes and monks who made copies of the original manuscripts changed the texts down the years, and, therefore, no one would really know for sure if these were the true words of Christ." I would ask you if you have evidence to back your claim. What if I said that I didn't think Mark Twain really wrote *Huckleberry Finn*, and I accused him of plagiarizing the whole thing? You see, I can make that argument all day long, but it is mere opinion if I do not provide you with evidence. Where is the evidence that medieval monks tampered with the original?

Furthermore, do you have any knowledge in the field of textual criticism? Let's look at Plato, for example. Does anyone doubt that the words we read from *The Republic* are indeed Plato's words? Probably not. What about the history of the manuscript? Well, Plato wrote it in about 355 B.C., and the earliest manuscript we have is from 900 A.D. That's a gap of close to twelve centuries, for those of you keeping score at home. Let's take the Scriptures, specifically the New Testament. It was written between 50 and 90 A.D., and the earliest manuscripts we have are from 100 A.D. That's a gap of only 50 years. I hardly call that a significant amount of time for tweaking of epic proportions (pun intended). What would have been the monks' motivation anyway?

The New Testament and The Old Testament—check out the Dead Sea Scrolls if you want more evidence—are reliable books of antiquity. Their historical credibility is verified not only through stout manuscript evidence, but also through continuing archaeological discoveries which support the evidence for the lives of the people and the events mentioned in their pages.

WHO IS YOUR ULTIMATE AUTHORITY?

Everyone has an ultimate standard by which he or she makes sense out of the world. This ultimate standard may be empiricism ("Seeing is believing.") or rationalism ("I think, therefore, I am."). These two standards fall under the umbrella of this premise: Everyone is his or her own authority and, as such, is free to decide for himself or herself what is true.

But suppose for a moment there is a God who is the sovereign Creator—the Eternal, the All-powerful, and the All-knowing. Could you think of any higher authority than this God? What kind of God would He be if He needed a mere man or a mere man's philosophy to vouch for Him? He certainly wouldn't be very "God-like," would He? Therefore, wouldn't you expect this God to speak with self-attesting authority? Furthermore, who could authenticate His revelation to mankind? How could anyone know what this God would say and be like in order to confirm this revelation? It comes to this: **If you will not accept the Bible on its own terms, then what you are basically saying is that you will never accept a revelation from God. Only God, if He is God, could reveal Himself with final authority, and that is exactly what He does.** So those who reject the Bible reject it not for reasons of hard evidence, but simply because they have a different absolute measure by which they judge truth. I presuppose the Bible as my ultimate authority and foundation for truth, where they presuppose their own minds.

Questions to Consider

1. Before reading this chapter, did you believe the Bible was:

    a. The inspired, infallible word of God?
    b. Simply good principles to live by?
    c. Merely legend passed down through the years?
    d. Good firewood?

    Explain your answer.

2. After having read the chapter, has your position changed? Why or why not?

3. Do you believe in the supernatural? Explain why or why not.

CHAPTER 7

Back to Barbecue

Bert – "So why are you dressed up?"

Earnest – "I went to church this morning."

Bert – "What kind of church?"

Earnest – "It's non-denominational—just a Christian church."

Bert – "Interesting. So I had no idea you were a Bible-thumper," he chuckles.

Earnest – "Well, I definitely believe in the Bible, but I'm not into pushing my beliefs on others."

Bert – "Good for you, man! I get so tired of those folks who feel the need to convert everybody. I think it just shows weakness on their part."

Earnest – "How so?"

Bert – "It just seems like they're afraid to stand alone—almost like they need affirmation for what they believe. We all have our own individual beliefs. What's true and right for one person isn't necessarily true for the next."

Earnest – "Hmm. So what do you believe?"

Bert – "I personally believe that if you are a good person, you're going to be alright, whatever your idea of 'alright' is. We're all here just trying to do our best, you know? To me, it shouldn't matter what path you take. None of us really *knows* what the truth is anyway. And if there really is a God, I can't imagine Him condemning people to 'hell' for not believing one particular way. That just wouldn't be fair. It makes me so mad when these self-righteous Christians claim they're the only ones going to 'heaven.' You say you're a Christian—do *you* really believe that Jesus Christ is the only way to God?"

Earnest – "Yes, I do."

Bert – "So you would condemn all the Jews, Muslims, Hindus, and the rest of the moral population to hell just because they don't see Jesus as the Son of God?"

Earnest – "I don't really think it's my place to condemn anyone to hell, but I do know that Jesus is 'the way, the truth, and the life.' The

Word of God says that it's only through His blood that any of us can get to the Father."

Bert – "Look, Earnest, any educated person knows that the Bible isn't really true. Evolution proved that a long time ago. I've read my fair share of the Bible, and, sure, we can glean a modicum of wisdom from its tales and proverbs, just like any other ancient writing, but do you honestly think that all that stuff really happened? The Bible is basically a bunch of myths. My grandmother was a Christian, and she used to tell us stories from the Bible. Let me ask you: how is a talking donkey plausible? (That one was my personal favorite.)"

Earnest – "It was a miracle."

Bert – "Miracles like that don't happen these days, and if they don't happen now, why would they have happened then?"

Earnest – "People are miraculously healed of all sorts of diseases all the time; how do you account for that?"

Bert – "They just got lucky in my opinion. What about all the people who don't get healed—people who've got entire churches praying for them? Why wouldn't God heal them? That seems so arbitrary."

Earnest – "Well, Bert, He's God—His ways are too lofty for us to understand."

Bert – "And you buy that? That is such a copout, Earnest. Figure something out for yourself. Give me a reason without regurgitating what you learned in Sunday school. Remember, I don't believe in the Bible. You can't keep using it for your arguments. Give me a rational explanation, please."

Earnest – "Well, I take the Bible as the foundation for all truth. Asking me to stop using it in my arguments is like asking someone to speak without vocal chords."

Bert – "Well, I guess we're done with our little discussion then," he says with a victorious laugh.

Earnest – "If you don't want to believe, it's your choice. I just want you to recognize what you're really claiming."

Bert – "What are you talking about?"

Earnest – "Recognize that in choosing to reject the Gospel, you are assuming the position of God in your own life."

Bert – "Okay, so what's wrong with that? It's my life, Earnest."

Earnest – "Well, if you are your own authority, then what will be your foundation for right and wrong, for morality and ethics?"

Bert – "I know what's right and wrong. I'm a good

person. I treat others as I like to be treated. I don't steal, kill, or covet my neighbor's wife," he snickers.

Earnest – "Okay, it's obvious that you're mocking me now by quoting from the Ten Commandments, but think about it . . . are you not borrowing from my Christian worldview to furnish ethics for your own?

Bert – "What?"

Earnest – "Let me put it this way: Can you come up with any 'moral' behavior that is not found directly in Scripture?"

Bert – "Hmm . . . I guess not. But so what? The Bible was written by men who just felt the same way I do."

Earnest – "But where does that morality come from, Bert?"

Bert – "From inside of us. I believe that all men desire in their heart of hearts to do good to their fellow man or at least to treat others as they'd like to be treated."

Earnest – "Wow, you must not watch the news. How do you account for evil in the world if all men are basically good?"

Bert – "I don't know . . . society is corrupt."

Earnest – "Come on, Bert, you're not going to pull the whole 'noble savage' thing on me

> now. Are you honestly saying that civilization is the culprit? Just know that if you take civilization away, all the good it's done will have to go too—advances in modern technology, medicine, etc."

Bert – "Well, I guess I don't know where evil comes from. Maybe some people are just innately bad."

Earnest – "You do realize that you're contradicting what you said thirty seconds ago . . . that all people are basically good?"

Bert – "I guess I just don't have it all figured out just yet. Maybe being *God* isn't as easy as I thought," he says with sarcasm.

Earnest – "That's why God is *God*, and we're not."

Well, I'd have to say Earnest did a lot better this time around. Bert may not have been altogether convinced, but Earnest definitely gave him something to chew on besides his brisket sandwich, and that's all that could be asked of him. Hopefully, Bert will come away from their discussion thinking a little bit more about what he really believes. If you consider yourself a skeptic, I hope you'll do the same after having read this book. I would challenge you to examine your own reasons for rejecting the Gospel and see what's at the root. In my experience, I've found that more than any of these other Bert-like reasons, there are three primary reasons people reject the Gospel.

Some reject Christ for "intellectual" reasons. If you are educated today in our public school system, if you go to college and get a degree, or if you're simply a consumer of mass media, then you have undoubtedly been fed the idea that becoming a Christian is equivalent to committing intellectual suicide. It goes something like this: "No thinking person, no intelligent person would ever believe in the Bible or in miracles or anything silly like that." I see and hear this way of thinking on many different talk shows, on TV, and in various kinds of literature on a daily basis. The truth of the matter is that some of the greatest minds in history and in our world today were and are "born-again" Christians. Those who so firmly hold to the belief that Christians are neither intelligent nor cultured have apparently never heard of J.R.R. Tolkien (well, now they have, thanks to Peter Jackson), C.S. Lewis, Dr. Hugh Ross, Dr. Bill Dembski, Dr. Michael Behe, or the many different Christian intellects, philosophers, astrophysicists, biologists, psychologists, psychiatrists, lawyers, authors, doctors, and artists. No, what they see are the debates on CNN, *Crossfire*, or on *Donahue*, with "Mr. or Ms. Two-PhDs-from-Harvard" against "Billy Bob, the Backwoods Baptist." We have all seen it; it goes something like this: "Well, Phil, God said it, I believe it, that settles it!" What results is this kind of cartoon character representation of what it means to be a Christian (and this person speaks for all Christians, of course) who is pitted against this very calm and rational intellectual. This only affirms the already prevalent idea that people of faith and people of facts are polar opposites. You can also watch a lot of the junk that passes for Christian TV, and the gold-leafed gospel that some (not all) of those people sell is enough to make me a skeptic. Unfortunately, these people only validate many of the "intellectual" reasons skeptics cite for rejecting the Good News.

Sometimes the reasons are of a psychological nature. I had a conversation with a professing atheist years ago, and I remember asking him, "Why don't you believe in God?" He went straight down the classic atheistic arguments for not believing in God, saying, "Well, first of all, there is so much evil and suffering in the world, how can anyone believe in God? If there is a God, He is not a good God. Second of all, look at science and evolution. Haven't they proven that the God of Scripture, the Christian God, is not true? We have no need for deity anymore. And look at the great diversity of religions and pluralistic belief systems that we have today. I mean, are you really saying all these people are wrong and you're right? What about the people who have never heard this message? What is going to happen to them?" After dialoging with him for a while on all these issues, I said this: "Mike," (which is not his name) "What was it like growing up in your house?" He said, "Well, I never really knew my dad. When I was two years old, he left us," and he went on to describe how his views of life and of love had been severely damaged by this one instance.

"Mike," I said, "I believe I can lead you to some answers to the questions and doubts you have about God and the Christian faith. By no means do I have all the answers, but I have books, and I know some people who have a lot more knowledge than I have, and I think they'll be able to help you out. But I believe that in the long run you're going to see that your real reason for rejecting God and Christ is not any of these other reasons you've brought up. You're going to see that when your dad left you as a kid, somehow, in your heart and your mind, God left you too."

The last and primary reason I believe people reject the Gospel is simply because they don't want it to be true. The fact is that God has revealed Himself to the world and to all of mankind. One way He has revealed Himself is through His creation. Another is through conscience—or a sense of morality—which He has woven into the fabric of every person. Everyone has an innate sense of right and wrong, as we spoke about in chapter two. As a man, I can account for that. So, in essence, many people take this innate knowledge of our God, our Creator, and try to suppress it because they simply don't want Him to exist. Like Bert, they don't want to have to answer to anyone but themselves. Take a look at what Aldous Huxley, author of the best-selling book, *Brave New World*, says in another of his books, *Ends and Means*:

> I had motives for not wanting the world to have a meaning; consequently I assumed that it had none, and was able without any difficulty to find satisfying reasons for this assumption . . . .For myself, as, no doubt, for most of my contemporaries, the philosophy of meaninglessness was essentially an instrument of liberation. The liberation we desired was simultaneously liberation from a certain political and economic system and liberation from a certain system of morality. We objected to the morality because it interfered with our sexual freedom . . . .[1]

Check out this quote from Thomas Nagel, a professor of philosophy at New York University:

> I want atheism to be true and am made uneasy by the fact that some of the most intelligent and well-informed people I know are religious believers. It isn't just that I don't believe in God and, naturally hope that I'm right in my belief. It's that I hope that there is no God! I don't want there to be a God; I don't want the universe to be like that.[2]

Why do they reject faith in God? These very intelligent, rational men boldly admit that they simply do not *want* to believe. I appreciate their honesty.

It comes to this: Acknowledging that there is a higher power than ourselves forces us to relinquish the autonomy we hold so dear. So here's the real question, dear reader: The lifestyle that you've chosen and the perspective that you're seeking to live out right now, is it working for you? Do you measure up to the standards you set for yourself? Do you feel shame and guilt when you don't? Do you find yourself longing for acceptance, but you're not sure from where? Do you have healthy intimate relationships, or is there a sense of disconnection? Is there a sense of emptiness no matter how many pleasures you have or how much power you attain? Do you truly have meaning and purpose in your life? Do you have joy and peace? God is saying to you and to me: "Come to my Son, and I will set you free. Stop trying to go it alone. It's not every man for himself. I've given myself for every man."

Notes

Chapter 2 - Because it's True for You, But Not for Me

[1] The Barna Research Group, Ltd., "Americans Are Most Likely to Base Truth on Feelings," *www.barna.org*, 12 Feb. 2002.

[2] Based on a story by Paul Copan found online.

[3] Nietzsche is conveniently paraphrased in Copan. Walter Kaufman, ed. and trans., "The Gay Science" in *The Portable Nietzsche* (New York, NY: Viking, 1954) 95.

Paul Copan, *True for You, But Not For Me* (Minneapolis, MN: Bethany House Publishers, 1998) 22.

Chapter 3 - Because all Paths Lead to God

[1] La Tonya Taylor, "The Church of O," *www.christianitytoday.com*, *Christianity Today*, Vol. 46, No. 4, p. 38, 1 April, 2002.

[2] T. Keller and C. Garland, *The Current Intellectual State of Affairs in America*: "Philosophical & Religious Pluralism," *www.monergism.com*, 20 June 2003.

Chapter 4 - Because all Christians are Hypocrites

[1] Facts 1–3 are loosely based on:

Frank Harber, *Reasons for Believing* (Green Forest, AR: New Leaf Press, 1998) 143–147.

Chapter 5 - Because Evolution is True

[1] Patrick Glynn, *GOD: The Evidence* (Rocklin, CA: Prima Publishing, 1997) 2–3.

[2] Definition of Intelligent Design, "Intelligent Design and the Theory of Evolution," *www.wordiq.com*, 2004.

[3] A quote from Stephen J. Gould, courtesy of David Friend and the editors of *Life Magazine*, "The Meaning of Life" (1991) 33, as quoted in Ravi Zacharias, *Can Man Live With-*

out God (Nashville, TN: W Publishing Group, 1994) 31.

[4] Taken from Dr. James Tour's résumé at *www.jmtour.com*, last updated 16 September 2004.

[5] Taken from Dr. William Dembski's résumé at *www.iscid.org*, last updated 2003.

Chapter 6 - Because the Bible is Full of Myths

[1] Peter Kreeft, *Between Heaven and Hell* (Madison, WI: InterVarsity Press, 1982) 75–80.

[2] Science Fair Projects Encyclopedia Page, "Correlation implies causation (logical fallacy)," *www.all-science-fair-projects.com*, last updated 20 September 2004.

Chapter 7 - Back to Barbecue

[1] Aldous Huxley, *Ends and Means: An Inquiry into the Nature of Ideas and into the Methods Employed for Their Realization* (London/New York: Chatto & Windus/Harper & Brothers, 1937) 270–273.

[2] Thomas Nagel, as quoted by J. Budziszewski, "The Second Tablet Project," *First Things* 124 (June/July 2002): 28.

Recommended Reading

Always Ready by Dr. Greg Bahnsen

Between Heaven and Hell by Peter Kreeft

God, the Evidence by Patrick Glynn

Miracles by C.S. Lewis

Reasons for Believing by Dr. Frank Harber

Relativism by Francis Beckwith and Gregory Koukl

The Case for Faith, by Lee Strobel

"The Great Debate: Does God Exist?" Dr. Greg Bahnsen vs. Dr. Gordon Stein (listen online)

The Question of God: C.S. Lewis and Sigmund Freud Debate God, Love, Sex, and the Meaning of Life by Dr. Armand Nicholi, Jr.

The Universe Next Door by James Sire

"*True For You, But Not For Me*" by Paul Copan

To order additional copies of

WHY BERT'S NOT A CHRISTIAN

Have your credit card ready and call:

1-877-421-READ (7323)

or please visit our web site at
www.pleasantword.com

Also available at:
www.amazon.com
and
www.barnesandnoble.com